ITALY 2016 HUMAN RIGHTS REPORT

EXECUTIVE SUMMARY

The Italian Republic is a multiparty parliamentary democracy with a bicameral parliament consisting of the Chamber of Deputies and the Senate. The constitution vests executive authority in the Council of Ministers, headed by a prime minister whose official title is President of the Council of Ministers. The President of the Republic, who is the head of state, nominates the prime minister after consulting with political party leaders in parliament. International observers considered the national parliamentary elections in 2013 to be free and fair.

Civilian authorities maintained effective control over the security forces.

As of December 7, more than 175,100 migrants and refugees had arrived in the country during the year, more than the previous peak in 2014. The continued elevated flow of migrants and refugees into the country overwhelmed the government's capability to host asylum seekers and unaccompanied minors. Migrants and refugees lived in often inadequate or substandard shelters for extended periods and were vulnerable to forced labor and other abuses; unaccompanied minors were particularly at risk. Corruption remained a significant problem.

Other human rights problems included excessive and abusive police use of force, prison overcrowding and incarceration of pretrial detainees with convicted criminals, substandard prisons, the slow pace of justice, abuse of libel laws to stifle criticism of public officials, domestic violence, cases of female genital mutilation and cutting (FGM/C), abuse of children, child pornography, and anti-Semitic hate speech online. Persons were subjected to both labor and sex trafficking. Societal prejudice and municipal government policies resulted in the mistreatment of minorities, including Roma, exacerbating their social exclusion and restricting access to education, health care, employment, and other social services. Observers also reported cases of violence and discrimination against lesbian, gay, bisexual, transgender, and intersex (LGBTI) persons. Forced labor, labor exploitation, and child labor were problems, especially prevalent in the service sector and agriculture. There was employment discrimination based on ethnicity, gender, religion, disability, sexual orientation, and gender identity.

The government investigated, prosecuted, and punished officials who committed crimes and abuses whether in the security forces or elsewhere in the government. Impunity sometimes existed.

Section 1. Respect for the Integrity of the Person, Including Freedom from:

a. Arbitrary Deprivation of Life and other Unlawful or Politically Motivated Killings

There were some reports that security forces committed arbitrary or unlawful killings. On July 13, a Florence court sentenced three Carabinieri officers, Vincenzo Corni, Stefano Castellano, and Agostino Della Porta, to seven to eight months in prison for manslaughter in the death of Riccardo Magherini, which occurred during his arrest in 2014. The court found the three officers handcuffed and held Magherini in a position that hindered his ability to breathe.

Another Carabinieri officer was under investigation in Padua for the killing of Mauro Guerra in July 2015. Guerra suffered from a psychological disorder and had demonstrated aggressive behavior. His parents had requested police assistance, which Guerra was fleeing when he assaulted an officer.

b. Disappearance

There were no reports of politically motivated disappearances.

c. Torture and Other Cruel, Inhuman, or Degrading Treatment or Punishment

The constitution and law prohibit such practices. Nongovernmental organizations (NGOs) and international organizations highlighted the lack of a law criminalizing torture as a loophole in the judicial system. Under existing law, prosecution for torture may occur only if the victim comes forward to accuse the perpetrator of an assault.

On January 20, a Genoa court ordered the Ministry of Justice to pay 4,300 euros ($4,700) and 4,900 euros ($5,400) to two detainees held in overcrowded cells in Milan, Cremona, Marassi, and Chiavari.

Prison and Detention Center Conditions

Prison and detention center conditions mostly met international standards, but some prisons were significantly overcrowded and antiquated.

Physical Conditions: On September 30, the Ministry of Justice reported 54,465 inmates were held in 193 prisons designed to hold a total 49,796 persons. Overall the system was at 109 percent of capacity, but in some prisons overcrowding was severe: Como (176 percent), Brescia (175 percent), and Larino, in the province of Campobasso (174 percent). The law requires the separation of pretrial detainees from convicted prisoners, but authorities sometimes held both in the same sections of prison facilities. According to Ristretti Orizzonti, a website of an NGO that tracks information on incarceration, between January 1 and October 14, 27 prisoners committed suicide, and another 48 died of natural causes.

The regional governments of Tuscany and Sicily failed to implement fully a 2014 law requiring them to create special centers for detainees with psychiatric disorders by March 2015 to replace two existing judiciary psychiatric hospitals considered inadequate by the government and international observers. The facilities hosted 37 inmates on September 13.

Administration: On July 4, the Ministry of Justice reported that 732 prisoners, mostly serving sentences related to organized crime or terrorism, were subject to special limitations on their interactions with other prisoners, as well as their own relatives.

Independent Monitoring: The government permitted independent human rights organizations, parliamentarians, and the media to visit prisons and detention centers. The government also provided representatives of the Office of the UN High Commissioner for Refugees (UNHCR) and NGOs access to detention centers for migrants and refugees in accordance with UNHCR's standard modalities. On April 8-21, a delegation from the Council of Europe's Committee for the Prevention of Torture visited the country. As of year's end, the report of the delegation's visit was not yet published.

d. Arbitrary Arrest or Detention

The constitution prohibits arbitrary arrest and detention, and the government generally observed these prohibitions.

Role of the Police and Security Apparatus

The National Police and the Carabinieri maintain internal security. The Carabinieri are the national military police. Although it is also one of the five branches of the armed forces, it carries out certain civilian law enforcement duties. The Ministry of Interior coordinates between the National Police and nonmilitary units of the Carabinieri. The army is responsible for external security but also has specific domestic security responsibilities, such as guarding public buildings. The three other police forces are the Prison Police, which operates the prison system; the National Forestry Corps, which enforces law in parks and forests; and the Financial Police, the customs agency under the Ministry of Economy.

Civilian authorities maintained effective control over the National Police and the Carabinieri, and the government has effective mechanisms to investigate and punish abuse and corruption. There were no reports of impunity involving the security forces during the year, although long delays by prosecutors and other authorities in completing some investigations reduced the effectiveness of mechanisms to investigate and punish police abuses.

Arrest Procedures and Treatment of Detainees

To detain an individual, police must have a warrant issued by a public prosecutor, unless a criminal act is in progress or there is a specific and immediate danger to which police officers must respond. The law requires authorities to inform a detainee of the reason for arrest. If authorities detain a person without a warrant, an examining prosecutor must decide within 24 hours of detention whether there is enough evidence to request the validation of the arrest. The investigating judge then has 48 hours to confirm the arrest and recommend whether to prosecute. In cases of alleged terrorist activity, authorities may hold suspects up to 48 hours before bringing the case to a magistrate. These rights were generally respected.

There is no provision for bail, but judges may grant provisional liberty to detainees awaiting trial. The government provides a lawyer at government expense to indigent persons. The law requires authorities to allow a detainee to see an attorney within 24 hours, or within 48 hours in cases of suspected terrorist activities. In exceptional circumstances, usually in cases of organized crime or when there is a risk that attorneys may attempt to tamper with evidence, the investigating judge may take up to five days to interrogate the accused before allowing access to an attorney. The law permits family members access to detainees.

<u>Pretrial Detention</u>: Lengthy pretrial detention and trial delays were a problem. In September, 34 percent of all prisoners were in either pretrial detention or awaiting a final sentence. The maximum term of pretrial detention is two to six years, depending on the severity of the alleged crime. According to independent analysts and magistrates, delays resulted from the large number of drug and immigration cases awaiting trial, the lack of judicial remedies, and the presence of more than 18,000 foreign detainees. In some cases they could not be placed under house arrest because they had no legal residence, and the insufficient distribution of offices and resources, including shortages of judges and staff.

<u>Detainee's Ability to Challenge Lawfulness of Detention before a Court</u>: Persons who have been arrested or detained are entitled to challenge in front of a judge the legal basis or arbitrary nature of their detention. If the grounds on which they were arrested are found insufficient, they are granted prompt release. Persons found to have been unlawfully detained are able to request compensation. As a safeguard against unjustified detention, detainees may request a panel of judges (a liberty tribunal) to review their cases on a regular basis to determine whether to continue the detention.

e. Denial of Fair Public Trial

The constitution provides for an independent judiciary, and the government generally respected judicial independence. There were isolated reports that judicial corruption and politically motivated investigations by magistrates impeded justice. A significant number of court cases involved long trial delays.

Trial Procedures

The constitution provides for the right to a fair public trial, and an independent judiciary generally enforced this right. Defendants have the right to the presumption of innocence and to be informed promptly and in detail of the charges against them as well as access to interpretation or translation services, as needed. Trials are fair and public, but they can be delayed. Defendants have the right to be present at their trials.

The courts of assizes, which have jurisdiction in the initial trial for the most serious crimes, consist of two professional judges and six laypersons chosen at random from among citizens between the ages of 30 and 65. The law provides for defendants to have access to an attorney of their choice in a timely manner, or have one provided at public expense if they are unable to pay. Defendants had adequate time to discuss and prepare cases with their lawyers in appropriate facilities available in all prisons. Prosecutors must make evidence available to all defendants and their attorneys upon request. All defendants have the right to confront and question witnesses against them and to present witnesses and evidence on their own behalf. Defendants may not be forced to testify or confess guilt, and they have a right to appeal verdicts. These rights extend to all defendants.

Domestic and European institutions continued to criticize the slow pace of the judicial process. On May 3, the Ministry of Justice reported that the first trial of civil cases lasted an average of 367 days. The country's "prescription laws" (statutes of limitations) in criminal proceedings require that a trial must end by a certain date. Courts determine when the statute of limitations should apply. Defendants often took advantage of delays in proceedings in order to exceed the statute of limitations. By doing so they could avoid a guilty sentence at trial or gain release pending an appeal.

Political Prisoners and Detainees

There were no reports of political prisoners or detainees.

Civil Judicial Procedures and Remedies

By law individuals and organizations may seek civil remedies for human rights violations through domestic courts. Individuals may bring a case of alleged human rights violations by the government to the European Court of Human Rights once they exhaust all avenues for a remedy in the country's court system. According to the Ministry of Justice, in 2015 the average length of civil judicial proceedings, including appeals, was 86 months.

f. Arbitrary or Unlawful Interference with Privacy, Family, Home, or Correspondence

The law prohibits such actions, and there were some reports that the government failed to respect these prohibitions. The Supreme Court's lead prosecutor may authorize wiretaps of terrorism suspects at the request of the prime minister. According to independent observers, prosecutors did not always limit the use of wiretaps to cases of absolute necessity as the Supreme Court required. The law allows magistrates to destroy illegal wiretaps that police discover or to seize transcripts of recordings that are irrelevant to the judicial case or are from commercial eavesdropping.

The press reported that in 2015 the government spent more than 200 million euros ($220 million) for wiretapping. On February 26, Palermo prosecutors requested the indictment of the authors of an article published by the weekly magazine *L'Espresso* containing alleged transcripts of wiretapped calls in which the regional president of Sicily, Rosario Crocetta, was involved.

Section 2. Respect for Civil Liberties, Including:

a. Freedom of Speech and Press

The constitution provides for freedom of speech and press, and the government generally respected these rights. An independent press, an effective judiciary, and a functioning democratic political system combined to provide for freedom of speech and press.

Freedom of Speech and Expression: Speech inciting violence based on racial, ethnic, national, or religious discrimination is a crime punishable by up to 18 months in prison. On July 13, legislation making Holocaust denial an aggravating circumstance in judicial proceedings against such speech entered into force. No convictions were reported during the year.

The law considers insults against any divinity to be blasphemy, a crime punishable by a fine ranging from 51 to 309 euros ($56 to $340). There were no reports regarding enforcement of these laws during the year.

Press and Media Freedoms: Laws that restrict freedom of speech apply to the print media as well. The independent media were active and expressed a wide variety of views. There was frequent political debate over the threat posed by bias and partisanship on the part of some of the country's leading media outlets. Through his family holding company, Fininvest, former prime minister Silvio Berlusconi held a controlling share in the country's largest private television company, Mediaset; its largest magazine publisher, Mondadori; and its largest advertising company, Publitalia. Berlusconi's brother owned one of the country's nationwide daily newspapers, *Il Giornale*. Media organizations tended to reflect the point of view of their proprietors or backers, whether a business entity or a political group.

<u>Libel/Slander Laws</u>: Journalists face prison sentences of up to six years if convicted of libel. Public officials continued to bring cases against journalists under libel laws. On July 16, a judge in Milan convicted a journalist, Antonio Rossitto, and the editor of the magazine *Panorama*, Giorgio Mule, and ordered them to pay 800 euros ($880) as a fine and 45,000 euros ($49,500) as compensation to Sicilian Governor Crocetta, who sued them for defamation. In 2012 the magazine published an article alleging links between Crocetta and organized crime gangs.

<u>Nongovernmental Impact</u>: The National Federation of the Italian Press reported some instances of threats against journalists made by members of criminal organizations. On February 12, police arrested Gionbattista Ventura, boss of an organized crime clan, for repeatedly threatening Paolo Borrometi, a reporter who had written articles on the Ventura clan's activities in the province of Ragusa.

Internet Freedom

The government did not restrict or disrupt access to the internet or censor online content, and there were no credible reports that the government monitored private online communications without appropriate legal authority. The National Center for the Fight against Child Pornography, a special unit of the postal and communications division of the National Police, monitored websites for crimes involving child pornography. According to International Telecommunication Union statistics, 66 percent of the population used the internet in 2015, and 24 percent had a fixed broadband subscription.

Academic Freedom and Cultural Events

There were no government restrictions on academic freedom or cultural events.

b. Freedom of Peaceful Assembly and Association

The constitution provides for the freedoms of assembly and association, and the government generally respected these rights.

c. Freedom of Religion

See the Department of State's *International Religious Freedom Report* at www.state.gov/religiousfreedomreport/.

d. Freedom of Movement, Internally Displaced Persons, Protection of Refugees, and Stateless Persons

The constitution provides for freedom of internal movement, foreign travel, emigration, and repatriation, and the government generally respected these rights.

<u>Abuse of Migrants, Refugees, and Stateless Persons</u>: Representatives of UNHCR, the International Organization for Migration (IOM), and other humanitarian organizations condemned alleged abuse of minors who were seeking asylum, prolonged periods of their detention, and their inadequate access to cultural mediators and lawyers. Mixed populations of refugees and migrants often remained in reception centers longer than the 35-day limit set by law. NGOs, including Parsec, On the Road, and Save the Children, claimed some of the Nigerian women detained in expulsion centers were victims of trafficking. Amnesty International (AI) reported isolated incidents of alleged abuse of migrants and refugees who refused to submit to identification procedures at ports of entry.

The IOM, UNHCR, and NGOs reported instances of labor exploitation of asylum seekers, especially in agriculture and in the service sector (see section 7.b.), and sexual exploitation of unaccompanied minors (see section 6, Children).

On July 8, approximately 200 migrants and refugees occupied a highway near Rome to protest poor living conditions at the shelter where they were staying and the long delays in processing asylum claims. During the year asylum seekers also staged protests against substandard living conditions and protracted asylum processes at shelters for asylum seekers in Messina, Salerno, and Bari.

On September 11, the magazine *L'Espresso* reported substandard conditions in a large reception center for asylum seekers in Foggia. According to the report, the center, which was managed by a cooperative on contract with the Ministry of Interior, hosted more than 1,000 persons, even though it was intended to house 636. Protection by guards effectively covered limited parts of the complex; the report's author claimed to have entered through a hole in the fence and spent seven days inside. The report stated that some asylum seekers housed in the complex slept in exterior courtyards, at times with stray dogs. Nigerian gangs reportedly infiltrated the complex and forced some female residents to prostitute themselves. Illicit labor recruiters allegedly hired several men inside to work on nearby farms for 15 euros ($17) per day, less than other migrants and refugees who lived outside the center were paid for work in the area.

On November 3, AI published a report describing isolated incidents in which police allegedly used excessive force to compel arriving migrants and asylum seekers to submit to identification procedures at ports of entry.

The government cooperated with UNHCR and other humanitarian organizations in providing protection and assistance to refugees, asylum seekers, stateless persons, and other persons of concern.

Protection of Refugees

Access to Asylum: The law provides for the granting of asylum or refugee status, and the government has established a system for providing protection to refugees. NGOs and independent observers identified difficulties in asylum procedures, including inconsistency of standards applied in reception centers and insufficient rates of referral of trafficking victims and unaccompanied minors to adequate services.

During the year high numbers of migrants and refugees arrived in the country, overwhelming the system for granting asylum. Between January 1 and October 31, the government received 98,477 asylum requests, processed 75,960 requests, and denied asylum or other forms of legal protection to 47,456 persons.

Between January 1 and November 28, a total of 24,235 unaccompanied minors arrived in the country. As of September 30, 14,225 unaccompanied minors were hosted in protected communities (see section 6, Children).

Safe Country of Origin/Transit: The country is party to the EU's Dublin III Regulation and its subsequent revisions, whereby members generally transferred asylum applications to the first EU member country in which the applicant arrived, or returned applicants to safe countries of origin.

Freedom of Movement: The law permits authorities to detain migrants and asylum seekers in centers for identification and expulsion for up to 90 days if authorities decide they pose a threat to public order or are a risk of escaping from an expulsion order or pre-expulsion jail sentence. In 2015 approximately 400 foreigners were held in nine centers. More than 25 percent requested asylum.

Employment: Asylum seekers may work legally two months after submitting an asylum request. Employers continued to discriminate against noncitizens in the labor market, taking advantage of insufficient enforcement of legal protection for noncitizens against exploitation.

Access to Basic Services: Authorities set up temporary centers to house mixed-migrant populations, including refugees and asylum seekers, but could not keep pace with the high number of arrivals and the increased number of asylum claims. The government's system of reception centers and shelters for asylum seekers was stretched beyond capacity. As of December 7, more than 175,100 persons were housed in sites throughout the country. Approximately 13 percent were housed in centers run directly by local authorities, generally considered of high quality, while the rest were in centers whose quality varied greatly and included many repurposed facilities such as old schools, military barracks, and apartments in residential buildings. NGOs reported thousands of legal and irregular foreigners, including migrants and refugees, lived in abandoned buildings in Rome and other major cities and had limited access to public services. The press reported limited health care, inadequate and overcrowded facilities, and a lack of access to legal counseling and basic education. Representatives of UNHCR, the IOM, and other humanitarian organizations denounced inhuman living conditions, in particular overcrowding, in some reception centers.

Durable Solutions: The government generally attempted to provide for integration and resettlement of refugees, with mixed results. Formal efforts to integrate refugees into the country's society were limited. In addition high unemployment limited the possibility of legal employment for large numbers of refugees. The government distributed asylum seekers throughout the country and provided shelter and services while their requests were processed, as well as some resettlement services after granting asylum. The government assisted migrants and refugees who opted to return to their home countries in cooperation with the IOM. Regional adjudication committees took from six to 15 months to process asylum claims, depending on the region. When legal appeals were taken into account, the process could last up to two years.

In July the IOM settled in the country 12 refugee families consisting of 48 persons from Sudan as part of the first movements from Sudan under the government's refugee resettlement quota system adopted in 2015.

Temporary Protection: The government also provided protection to individuals who may not qualify as refugees. Between January and October, the government provided humanitarian protection to 15,001 persons and subsidiary protection to 9,356 persons.

Section 3. Freedom to Participate in the Political Process

The constitution provides citizens the ability to choose their government in free and fair periodic elections held by secret ballot and based on universal and equal suffrage.

Elections and Political Participation

<u>Recent Elections</u>: National and international observers considered the parliamentary elections in 2013 to be free and fair.

<u>Participation of Women and Minorities</u>: No laws limit the participation of women and members of minorities in the political process, and women and minorities did so.

Section 4. Corruption and Lack of Transparency in Government

The law provides criminal penalties for corruption by officials. The government usually implemented these laws effectively, but officials sometimes engaged in corrupt practices with impunity. There were incidents of government corruption during the year.

<u>Corruption</u>: According to the National Anticorruption Authority, in 2015 citizens reported 3,000 cases of corruption to the authority as well as more than 1,400 instances of "insufficient transparency" of public offices. The Financial Police announced that in 2015 it arrested 177 persons and investigated approximately another 3,000 for abuse of power (56 percent), corruption (23 percent), and fraud (21 percent). Police reported irregularities in the implementation of almost 30 percent of audited public contracts in 2015.

On June 29, Rome prosecutors announced an investigation on 78 persons, including 11 public officials, three local politicians, and a leader of a Romani community, in a corruption case involving the management of camps for Romani families funded by the city of Rome.

<u>Financial Disclosure</u>: The law requires members of parliament to disclose their assets and incomes. The two chambers created a publicly accessible bulletin on each of their websites containing information on each parliamentarian, but only if the parliamentarian agrees to posting the information online. The law stipulates

that the presidents of the two chambers may order noncompliant members to submit the statements in 15 days but provides for no other sanctions. Ministers' disclosures must be posted online.

Public Access to Information: The law gives citizens the right to access government documents and to be informed of administrative processes. With some exceptions related to security, the government and local authorities respected this right for citizens, noncitizens, and the foreign press. The law was effectively implemented, but long delays in responding to requests were typical.

Section 5. Governmental Attitude Regarding International and Nongovernmental Investigation of Alleged Violations of Human Rights

A variety of domestic and international human rights groups generally operated without government restriction, investigating and publishing their findings on human rights cases. Government officials were cooperative and responsive to their views.

Government Human Rights Bodies: The Interministerial Committee for Human Rights at the Ministry of Foreign Affairs and the Senate's Human Rights Committee focused on international and high-profile domestic cases. The National Office to Combat Racial Discrimination (UNAR), a part of the Department of Equal Opportunity of the Presidency of the Council of Ministers (the Prime Minister's Office), assisted victims of discrimination. In a monitoring report on the country published on June 7, the European Commission against Racism and Intolerance (ECRI) criticized the government for not respecting the independence of UNAR and for providing the agency with insufficient resources to intervene in cases of discrimination.

Section 6. Discrimination, Societal Abuses, and Trafficking in Persons

Women

Rape and Domestic Violence: The prescribed penalty for rape, including spousal rape, is five to 12 years in prison. The law criminalizes the physical abuse of women (including by family members), provides for the prosecution of perpetrators of violence against women, and helps shield abused women from publicity. Judicial protective measures for violence occurring within a family allow for an ex parte application to a civil court judge in urgent cases. Police officers and judicial authorities prosecuted perpetrators of violence against women, but survivors frequently declined to press charges due to fear, shame, or ignorance of the law. A specific law on stalking includes mandatory detention for acts of sexual violence, including by partners. The law leaves responsibility for the provision of shelter to victims with local municipalities, some of which did not provide sufficient funds for shelters.

Between March 2014 and March 2015, authorities received 3,624 reports of cases of sexual violence, of which 91 percent were against women, and 11,223 cases of domestic violence, of which 82 percent were against women. According to a study by the independent research center Demoskopika released in March, almost 23,000 cases of violence against women occurred between 2010 and 2014, of which 6,000 were against minors. Between January 2015 and May 2016, 155 women were killed by their partners or former partners. Police arrested almost 22,000 persons accused of these crimes.

The Department of Equal Opportunity operated a hotline for victims of violence seeking immediate assistance and temporary shelter. The department also operated a hotline for victims of stalking. Between January and June, the department received approximately 16,600 calls, of which women placed 90 percent. The Ministry of Interior reported it received 9,875 complaints for stalking between January and July, 78 percent of which were made against men. Police took action against 1,385 perpetrators and in 285 cases ordered stalkers to leave the municipalities where victims lived.

Female Genital Mutilation/Cutting (FGM/C): FGM/C was a problem in some immigrant communities. It is a crime punishable by up to 12 years' imprisonment. Most of the mutilations were performed outside the country. Some victims were subjected to infibulation by relatives, very often without anesthesia or with rudimentary scalpels. Experts estimated that the increase in the number of new arrivals from the Gambia, Nigeria, Sudan, and Senegal resulted in an increase in the number of victims of FGM/C in migrant and refugee communities, but statistics were not available. The Department for Equal Opportunities operated a hotline for victims and other affected parties who requested the support of authorities and NGOs.

Sexual Harassment: Minor cases of verbal sexual harassment in public are punishable by up to six months' incarceration and a fine of up to 516 euros ($568). The government effectively enforced the law. By government decree, emotional abuse based on gender discrimination is a crime. Many victims failed to report incidents to authorities. Police investigated reports of harassment that were submitted to authorities.

Reproductive Rights: Couples and individuals have the right to decide the number, spacing, and timing of their children; manage their reproductive health; and have access to the information and means to do so, free from discrimination, coercion, and violence.

Discrimination: Women have the same legal status and rights as men. The government enforced laws prohibiting every form of discrimination in all sectors. There were reports of discrimination against women with respect to employment and occupation.

Children

Birth Registration: A child acquires citizenship automatically when the parents are citizens, when the parents of children born in the country's territory are unknown or stateless, or when the parents are foreigners whose countries of origin do not recognize the citizenship of their children born abroad. Citizenship is also granted if a child is abandoned in the country and in cases of adoption. Local authorities required immediate birth registration. Unaccompanied minors entering the country automatically receive a residence permit.

Child Abuse: In 2015 Telefono Azzurro, an NGO that advocates for children's rights, received calls reporting 2,680 cases of child abuse and 116 cases of missing children. An additional 2,067 cases were reported to a hotline of the Department of Equal Opportunity operated by Telefono Azzurro.

Early and Forced Marriage: The minimum age for marriage is 18, but juvenile courts may authorize marriages for individuals as young as 16. According to NGOs, hundreds of women were victims of forced marriages, especially among Asian and African immigrant communities.

Female Genital Mutilation/Cutting (FGM/C): See information in the women's section above.

Sexual Exploitation of Children: Authorities enforced the laws prohibiting sexual exploitation, the sale of children, offering or procuring a child for prostitution, and practices related to child pornography. Independent observers and the government estimated at least 2,500 foreign minors were victims of sexual exploitation. In

2015 authorities arrested 68 persons accused of exploiting minors for prostitution and investigated another 370 persons.

Between January 2015 and April 12, the National Center for the Fight against Child Pornography, a special unit within the postal and communications division of the National Police, monitored 23,981 websites and shut down 1,849. Authorities reported 574 persons to prosecutors and arrested 79 for crimes involving online child pornography. On August 23, police, in collaboration with Europol and authorities from 24 EU member states, arrested 75 persons suspected of establishing an international network to share child pornography and put another 100 under investigation.

The minimum age for consensual sex varies from 13 to 16, based on the relationship between partners.

Displaced Children: The Ministry of Interior reported that, between January and October 10, approximately 10,300 unaccompanied minors arrived in the country. As of August 31, approximately 8,900 were hosted in protected communities. Of the total, 23 percent were Egyptians, 15 percent Albanians, and 10 percent Gambians.

International Child Abductions: The country is a party to the 1980 Hague Convention on the Civil Aspects of International Child Abduction. See the Department of State's *Annual Report on International Parental Child Abduction* at travel.state.gov/content/childabduction/en/legal/compliance.html.

Anti-Semitism

There were approximately 30,000 Jews in the country. Anti-Semitic societal prejudices persisted. Some extremist fringe groups were responsible for anti-Semitic remarks and actions, including vandalism and publication of anti-Semitic material on the internet.

The Observatory on Anti-Semitism of the Foundation of Contemporary Jewish Documentation reported that on May 22, an unknown person punched a Jewish boy scout after shouting anti-Semitic insults against a group of scouts in Milan.

In its *Spring 2016 Global Attitudes Survey* released on July 11, the Pew Research Center reported that 24 percent of respondents in the country held an unfavorable opinion of the Jewish minority, compared to 69 percent who held an unfavorable opinion of Muslims and 82 percent who held an unfavorable opinion of Roma in the country. The report primarily explored European public opinion related to migration and terrorism but highlighted negative perceptions of other minority groups across the continent.

Anti-Semitic slogans and graffiti appeared in some cities, including Rome and Viareggio. Internet hate speech and bullying were the most common forms of anti-Semitic attacks, according to the Center for Jewish Contemporary Documentation.

Trafficking in Persons

See the Department of State's *Trafficking in Persons Report* at www.state.gov/j/tip/rls/tiprpt/.

Persons with Disabilities

The law prohibits discrimination against persons with physical, sensory, intellectual, and mental disabilities in employment, education, air travel and other transportation, access to health care, the judicial system, and the provision of other government services. The government enforced these provisions, but there were incidents of societal and employment discrimination.

Although the law mandates access to government buildings for persons with disabilities, physical barriers, particularly in public transit, continued to pose challenges, especially in the south. Many cities lacked infrastructure (such as subway elevators, cable railway stations, and ramps on sidewalks) for persons using wheelchairs or with limited mobility. Many municipalities provided free transportation to persons with disabilities who requested it.

National/Racial/Ethnic Minorities

Societal violence and discrimination against Roma, Sinti, Caminanti, and other ethnic minorities remained a problem. In its June 7 report on the country, ECRI asserted, "The law does not criminalize discrimination on grounds of color or language, and the penalties provided for are not always an effective, proportionate and dissuasive response to offenses involving racism and racial discrimination." In 2014 the National Office to Combat Racial Discrimination received 252 cases of alleged discrimination based on race or ethnicity; prosecutors opened investigations of the alleged perpetrators in 99 cases. There were reports of discrimination in occupation and employment based on race or ethnicity.

The press and NGOs reported cases of demagoguery, violent attacks, forced evictions from unauthorized camps, municipal mistreatment, and government efforts to remove Romani children from their parents. In its June 7 report, ECRI expressed concerns about the lack of uniformity in the integration of foreigners and Romani communities and the delays in the implementation of the 2012 Strategy on the Integration of Roma, Sinti, and Caminanti Communities. In particular, ECRI found the segregation of Romani communities in special camps and the inadequate living conditions there constituted a violation of human rights. It quoted a report by UNAR and the Association of Italian Municipalities released in October 2015 that almost 80 percent of Roma in the major cities lived in settlements, 36 percent of which were not authorized. The NGO Sant'Egidio estimated that between 120,000 and 150,000 Roma, 70,000 of whom were citizens, were concentrated on the fringes of urban areas in the central and southern parts of the country.

According to the NGO Associazione 21 Luglio, housing remained a serious concern for 35,000 Roma, most of whom were foreigners. Some of them, including elderly persons and persons with disabilities, were evicted from illegal encampments by local authorities that did not always provide adequate housing. On June 24, AI and other NGOs condemned the transfer by local authorities of 75 Romani families (approximately 300 persons) from a camp in Giuliano, near Naples, to a former fireworks factory (which exploded in 2015). Authorities decided to close the original camp, established in 2013, after reports surfaced it had been built near a toxic waste dump. AI claimed that the decision was a case of forced eviction, because the municipality did not consult the families before moving them to the new settlement, which lacked adequate facilities. AI reported that a representative of the local government asked the owners of mobile homes and recreational vehicles to make them available as living space for some families and that the new settlement provided only two portable toilets and four drinking fountains. Other families had to sleep in cars or in makeshift shacks.

Government officials at the national and local levels, including those from the Ministry of Interior and UNAR, met periodically with Roma and their representatives.

In a letter to Prime Minister Matteo Renzi on January 26, Nils Muiznieks, the human rights commissioner of the Council of Europe, expressed his concern about the continuing evictions of Roma, Sinti, and Caminanti as violations of the country's international commitments and domestic law.

On March 17, a Rome court recognized the right to citizenship of a Romani woman of Bosnian origin born in Italy. The court argued that as a minor she was not responsible for not having met the rules on citizenship and had the right to apply for citizenship when she reached age 18.

Acts of Violence, Discrimination, and Other Abuses Based on Sexual Orientation and Gender Identity

Antidiscrimination laws exist and apply specifically to LGBTI victims of homophobic and transphobic offenses. AI alleged the penalties for hate crimes based on sexual orientation and gender identity are not the same as for other kinds of hate crimes. There is no provision for a victim's sexual orientation to be considered an aggravating circumstance in hate crimes.

The press reported isolated cases of violence against gay and lesbian couples during the year. According to the NGO Arcigay, between May 2015 and May 2016, the media reported at least 104 cases of discrimination against members of the LGBTI community. On June 3, local press reported that a father in Alba attacked his son's partner and another friend, seriously injuring both. Reports attributed the attack to homophobia.

Since 2006 the Gay Help Line, an NGO that operated a hotline providing support to LGBTI persons, received an average 20,000 calls per year. Approximately 20 percent of callers under the age of 25 were minors, while 75 percent reported problems at school and with their families. Most adult callers (38 percent) reported cases of discrimination at work, while 30 percent reported being victims of violence.

On May 11, parliament adopted a measure establishing legal civil unions for same-sex couples.

Section 7. Worker Rights

a. Freedom of Association and the Right to Collective Bargaining

The law, including related regulations and statutes, provides for the right of workers to establish and join independent unions, bargain collectively, and conduct legal strikes. The government respected these rights. Antiunion discrimination is illegal, and employees fired for union activity have the right to request reinstatement, provided their employer has more than 15 workers in a unit or more than 60 workers in the country.

The law prohibits union organization of the armed forces and allows company and territorial-level agreements to deviate from the sectoral national collective agreements that regulate the working rights and conditions. The law mandates that strikes affecting essential public services (such as transport, sanitation, and health services) require longer advance notification and precludes multiple strikes within days of each other. The law allows only unions that represent at least half of the transit workforce to call a transit strike.

The government effectively enforced these laws. Employers who violate the law are subject to fines of up to 50,000 euros ($55,000), imprisonment for up to three months, or both. These penalties were generally sufficient to deter violations, although administrative and judicial procedures were sometimes subject to lengthy delays. Judges effectively sanctioned few cases of violations.

The government and employers generally respected freedom of association and the right to bargain collectively. Employers generally respected the rights of workers to organize and bargain collectively, although there were instances in which employers unilaterally annulled bargaining agreements. Employers continued to use short-term contracts and subcontracting to avoid hiring workers with bargaining rights.

b. Prohibition of Forced or Compulsory Labor

The law prohibits all forms of forced or compulsory labor, and the government effectively enforced the law. Resources and inspections were generally adequate. Penalties of eight to 20 years' imprisonment were sufficiently stringent. Actual sentences for forced and compulsory labor were significantly lower than those provided by law.

Forced labor occurred during the year. Workers were subjected to debt bondage in construction, domestic service, hotels, restaurants, and agriculture, especially in the south. Chinese men and women were forced to work in textile factories, and persons with disabilities from Romania and Albania were coerced into begging. On May 30, police assisted three Romanians who escaped from a pen on a sheep farm in the province of Sassari where their employer allegedly treated them as slaves. According to press reports, the employer seized the workers' cell phones, forced them to live in an unheated enclosure with the livestock, and physically abused them.

On May 18, parliament approved a law stiffening penalties for illicit middlemen and businesses that exploit agricultural workers. In particular new measures identify the conditions under which laborers might be considered exploited and include special programs in support of seasonal workers employed in agriculture.

There were reports that children were also subjected to forced labor (see section 7.c.).

Also see the Department of State's *Trafficking in Persons Report* at www.state.gov/j/tip/rls/tiprpt/.

c. Prohibition of Child Labor and Minimum Age for Employment

The law prohibits employment of children under the age of 16. There are specific restrictions on employment in hazardous or unhealthy occupations for minors, such as activities involving potential exposure to hazardous substances and gas, mining, excavations, and working with power-driven hoisting apparatus. Penalties for employing child labor include heavy fines or the suspension of a company's commercial activities. Government enforcement was generally effective in the formal economy. Enforcement was not effective in the relatively extensive informal economy, particularly in the south, where family-run businesses were common.

There were reports of child labor during the year. The number of irregular migrants between the ages of 15 and 18 entering the country from Libya and Egypt increased. Those that entered the informal labor market worked primarily in the manufacturing and service industries. In 2015 labor inspectors reported 187 cases of minors working illegally, 63 percent of whom worked in the service sector.

The Ministry of Labor, working with police and the Carabinieri, is responsible for enforcement of child labor laws, but its efforts produced limited results. As of September 30, the ministry identified 14,225 unaccompanied minors in the country, of whom 6,357 had escaped from their shelters. Of those assisted, 94 percent were boys and 81 percent were 16 or 17. The top three countries of origin for child laborers were Egypt, Albania, and Eritrea.

The Ministry of Labor recognized that unaccompanied minors were more vulnerable to child labor and worked to prevent exploitation by placing them in protected communities that provided education and other services.

d. Discrimination with Respect to Employment and Occupation

The law prohibits discrimination in employment based on race, color, sex, religion, political opinion, national origin or citizenship, social origin, disability, sexual orientation or gender identity, age, language, HIV-positive status, or other communicable diseases. The law requires equal pay for equal work. The government effectively enforced the law by imposing fines sufficient to deter violations.

There were reports of employment discrimination based on race or ethnicity. Unions criticized the government for providing insufficient resources to UNAR to intervene in all cases of discrimination and for the lack of adequate legal measures to address new types of discrimination.

Discrimination based on gender, religion, disability, sexual orientation, and gender identity also occurred. The government implemented some information campaigns, promoting diversity and tolerance, including in the workplace.

In many cases victims of discrimination were unwilling to request the forms of protections provided by employment laws or collective contracts. Women were underrepresented among chief judges and prosecutors. The Supreme Council of the Magistracy reported that, between September 2014 and March 9, only one quarter of newly appointed top magistrates and prosecutors were women, although more than half of all judges and prosecutors were women. The national authority monitoring the Milan stock market reported that in 2015 approximately 28 percent of the board members of listed companies were women. According to Eurostat, the salaries of women were on average 7.3 percent lower than those of men in similar jobs.

e. Acceptable Conditions of Work

The law does not provide for a minimum wage. Instead, collective bargaining contracts negotiated between unions and employers set minimum wage levels for different sectors of the economy. In 2015 the government set the official poverty line at 1,050.95 euros ($1,156.05) per month for a family of two. The legal workweek is 40 hours. Overtime work may not exceed two hours per day or an average of 12 hours per week. Unless limited by a collective bargaining agreement, the law sets maximum overtime hours in industrial firms at no more than 80 hours per quarter and 250 hours annually. The law prohibits compulsory overtime and provides for paid annual holidays. It requires rest periods of one day per week and 11 hours per day. Premium pay is required for overtime. The law sets basic health and safety standards and guidelines for compensation for on-the-job injuries. The law prohibits labor exploitation and illicit mediation.

The government, with regular union input, effectively enforced standards in the formal sector of the economy. Labor standards were only partially enforced in the informal sector. The Ministry of Labor is responsible for enforcement.

Resources, inspections, and remediation were generally adequate to ensure compliance in the formal sector only. Penalties for violations include up to six months' incarceration and fines of up to 6,400 euros ($7,040) but were not sufficient to deter all violations. In 2015 an adequate number of labor inspectors (3,119) and Carabinieri officers (324) inspected 145,697 companies identifying 41,570 undeclared workers, 1,716 illegal migrants, and 187 underage laborers. In 10,200 instances inspectors found violations of regulations on working hours and suspended 7,100 companies employing at least 20 percent of workers without a formal contract.

In 2015 the Financial Police identified 12,400 irregular workers and 11,300 informal workers, some of whom, especially undocumented migrants and asylum seekers, were victims of exploitation. Informal workers were often underpaid, worked in unhygienic conditions, or were exposed to safety hazards. Such practices occurred in the service, construction, and agricultural sectors.

On September 12, an independent research center, CGIA, estimated that there were 3.5 million irregular workers in the country, of whom 45 percent were employed as house cleaners and caregivers, 18 percent as agricultural laborers, 16 percent in bars and restaurants, and 15 percent in the construction sector.

In January the independent research center Eurispes reported that 28 percent of workers interviewed accepted employment without a regular contract. In particular, 80 percent of babysitters, 79 percent of tutors, and 72 percent of domestic workers operated under either informal or irregular arrangements.

According to unions, most of the workers in agriculture were at risk of exploitation. In 2015 the Ministry of Labor conducted an additional 8,662 inspections in southern regions identifying 2,524 irregular workers and 3,629 informal workers, shutting down the productive activities in 459 cases. In 2015 Carabinieri police arrested two recruiters charged with exploiting workers and placed another 14 recruiters under investigation.

In May the union-monitoring organization Observatory Placido Rizzotto reported that approximately 100,000 foreign workers were employed illegally in agriculture and were often exploited by illicit intermediaries. Most of them lacked adequate housing. According to the Ministry of Labor, the gap between the salaries of nationals and foreigners working in the country was 25 percent on average.

There were reports from some areas of Calabria, Puglia, Campania, and Sicily of significant numbers of informal foreign workers living and working temporarily or permanently in substandard or unsafe conditions.

According to the National Institute for Insurance against Accidents at Work, workers were generally able to remove themselves from dangerous health or safety conditions without jeopardizing their employment, and authorities protected employees in these situations.